Via Lucis

Stations of
The Resurrection

by
Fr Sabino Palumbieri

*All booklets are published thanks to the
generous support of the members of the
Catholic Truth Society*

CATHOLIC TRUTH SOCIETY
PUBLISHERS TO THE HOLY SEE

STATIONS

1- Jesus Rises from the Dead
2- The Disciples find the Tomb Empty
3- The Risen Lord Appears to Mary Magdalen
4- The Risen Lord Appears to Two Disciples on the Road to Emmaus
5- The Risen Lord Reveals Himself at the Breaking of Bread
6- The Risen Lord Appears to His Disciples
7- The Risen Lord Gives the Power to Forgive Sins
8- The Lord Confirms the Faith of Thomas
9- The Risen Lord Meets His Disciples on the shore of Galilee
10- The Risen Lord Confers Primacy on Peter
11- The Risen Lord Entrusts to His Disciples the Mission to the World
12- The Risen Lord Ascends to the Father
13- Waiting for the Holy Spirit with Mary the Mother of Jesus
14- The Risen Lord sends the Spirit Promised to the Disciples

Introduction

The Via Lucis is a response to the call of Vatican II to place a renewed importance on the Resurrection. Its inspiration lies in the spirituality of St John Bosco.

The text here translated was written by Fr Sabino Palumbieri, a Salesian, and the new devotion has been encouraged as part of the Jubilee celebrations in Rome: a shortened version of the Via Lucis was included in the official Jubilee Year prayer book.

The sculptures illustrated in this booklet are by Professor Giovanni Dragoni and can be found in at the Sanctuary of Our Lady of the Rosary, Pompeii, Italy.

Via Lucis
Stations of the Resurrection

Every station has three parts:

Each station begins with a passage from Holy Scripture (taken from the Jerusalem Bible)
Then follows the 1st meditation, which reflects upon and explains the scriptural text (First Meditation)
The 2nd meditation places the station in a modern context exploring its relevance for today (Second Meditation)
Depending on the time available one can either pray each station fully, or alternatively, choose only one of the meditations.

The Via Lucis can begin with a procession.

The procession can be led by three altar servers. One may carry the Easter candle; the other a book of the Gospels opened at the resurrection narrative; and the third, flowers as a sign of life or an icon of the Risen Christ.

The President of the assembly accompanies them; the Readers can remain at the lectern. The participants can either follow the stations around the church or remain seated.

OPENING PRAYER

A hymn may be sung during the opening procession

V   *In the name of the Father and of the Son and of the Holy Spirit*

R   *Amen*

Pr   Our lives are a ceaseless journey, a journey which we do not undertake alone. The Risen Lord has promised us: "I am with you always; yes, to the end of time" *(Mt 28:20)*. Our lives must be a journey of continual resurrection. We therefore come together, brothers and sisters, to acknowledge that our life is a Paschal journey together with the Risen Lord who is the light that guides our steps. A Scribe once said to Christ "I will follow you wherever you go" *(Mt 8:19)*. We follow Christ wherever he goes: first on the Via Crucis to Calvary and then on the Via Lucis. We will rediscover the Resurrection as the source of peace, the power of joy, the impetus behind all renewal. We will hear this Resurrection proclaimed from holy scripture, meditated upon in the light of our spiritual experience, and its meaning deepened by reflections rooted in the life of our own times, of our today, which is God's "today".

Pause for meditation

R   *Rejoice, Mother of the light:*
       Jesus sun of justice,
       Victorious over the darkness of the tomb,
       Brings light to the whole universe.
       Alleluia

Pr   *Let us Pray*

Pr   Father in heaven, pour out upon us your Spirit of light, that we may enter into the mystery of the Resurrection of your Only Begotten Son, who marks out the true destiny of all mankind. For death is not the end of everything, but the beginning of the newness of creation. The last word is yours, heavenly Father, you who bring us from death to life. Give us the Spirit of the Risen Lord and enable us to love, that we may become witnesses of his Resurrection.

R   *Amen*

❧ FIRST STATION ❧
JESUS RISES FROM THE DEAD

*"He has risen from the dead and now
he is going before you to Galilee;
it is there you will see him."*

❧ JESUS RISES FROM THE DEAD ❧

V   *We adore you and bless you O Risen Christ*
R   *Because by your death and resurrection you have given life to the world*

From the Gospel according to Matthew

After the Sabbath, and towards dawn on the first day of the week, Mary of Magdala and the other Mary went to visit the sepulchre. And all at once there was a violent earthquake, for the angel of the Lord, descending from heaven, came and rolled away the stone and sat on it. His face was like lightning, his robe white as snow. The guards were so shaken, so frightened of him, that they were like dead men. But the angel spoke; and he said to the women, 'There is no need for you to be afraid. I know you are looking for Jesus, who was crucified. He is not here, for he has risen, as he said he would. Come and see the place where he lay, then go quickly and tell his disciples, "He has risen from the dead and now he is going before you to Galilee; it is there you will see him". Now I have told you.' *(Mt 28:1-7)*

First Meditation

After the Sabbath, the feast begins. After the long wait in the gloom, the light shines. From the bosom of night a new dawn springs forth; a sunrise different from all others, the greatest of them all; the dawn of Easter. Bringing to birth a day which will never set. It ushers in the new man who was crucified, and who today is risen to live forever. The earthquake, the shining brightness of the garments, the light like that on the Mount of the Transfiguration - all signs that God is reavealing himself. He renews all things, rolling the stone away from the sepulchre: "now, I am making the whole of creation new" *(Ap 21:5)*. God is newness, he is beauty. A beauty which is always ancient and always new he is eternally young, and wants us to be young for all eternity. In baptism he gave us the seed of that same youth so that we can become heralds of his newness. The women go to the tomb, faithful to their master; they carry in their hands the ointment used to annoint and perfume the dead. The angel announces to them a new life: "Do not be afraid". Mankind has waited for this good news from the beginning: death is dead. Life springs into being.

Second Meditation

People of today still run the risk of hurrying to the tomb to embalm their own life. It is simpler to mourn for what is past than to look to the future. It is vital that we allow ourselves to be re-evangelised by the event ushered in by the dawn of that eternal day. Easter must be at the very centre of the "new evangelization" for our time. In this world where information flows so easily, we are in danger of letting the Paschal message be submerged by a flood of news stories. The Easter message must take its rightful place in the heart of every person and at the heart of the way they live their lives. Even the happiest news would count for nothing, if death had the final word.

All *Rejoice Virgin Mother:*
For Christ is risen.
Alleluia.

Pr Risen Lord, the world needs to be re-evangelized. Only a new evangelization can give peace to our hearts, bewildered by so many contradictory messages. Let your announcement ring out ever new. Let women everywhere be zealous messengers of the origin of new life: your resurrection. Renew us, implant in us a new mind, a new heart, new life. That we may think like you, love like you and prepare a future in harmony with your designs. Let us serve each other like you.

R *Amen*

All *O Mary, temple of the Holy Spirit,*
Guide us as witnesses of the Risen Lord
In the way of Light

⚉ SECOND STATION ⚉
THE DISCIPLES FIND THE TOMB EMPTY

'They have taken the Lord out of the tomb'
she said 'and we don't know
where they have put him.'

~ THE DISCIPLES FIND THE TOMB EMPTY ~

V   *We adore you and bless you O Risen Lord*
R   *Because by your death and resurrection you*
    have given life to the world

From the Gospel according to John

It was very early on the first day of the week and still dark, when Mary of Magdala came to the tomb. She saw that the stone had been moved away from the tomb and came running to Simon Peter and the other disciple, the one Jesus loved. 'They have taken the Lord out of the tomb' she said 'and we don't know where they have put him.'

So Peter set out with the other disciple to go to the tomb. They ran together, but the other disciple, running faster than Peter, reached the tomb first; he bent down and saw the linen cloths lying on the ground, but did not go in. Simon Peter who was following now came up, went right into the tomb, saw the linen cloths on the ground, and also the cloth that had been over his head; this was not with the linen cloths but rolled up in a place by itself. Then the other disciple who had reached the tomb first also went in; he saw and he believed. Till this moment they had failed to understand the teaching of scripture, that he must rise from the dead. *(Jn 20:1-9)*

First Meditation

What excitement there was around a grave. Seeing the stone rolled away, Mary of Magdala runs to the city. Peter and John hurry to the sepulchre where the body had been laid in haste, since the feast of Passover was close at hand *(Jn 19:42)*. There they saw an unusual scene for a new tomb: linen cloths on the ground and the sudarium put to one side. The troubled group of people gathered around the tomb, struggling to comprehend what had happened. What is new often provokes fear in us. John begins to believe in the omnipotence of God. God can if he wills; God can and will act. He can, because he is all-powerful. He wills because he is a Father. He acts because he is faithful. *(Jn 20:1-9)*

Second Meditation

People of today fear death and therefore try to remove it: but science, progress and technology merely push back the finishing line, and death in the end remains victorious.

Even though mankind has walked on the moon, its hopes are still swallowed up by the tomb. O what an unhappy story this would be, if the tomb in Jerusalem had succeeded in containing the Just One. It would have been the victory of Evil and not of Good, of darkness and not of light, of nothingness, not of being. If that senseless victory of death had taken place in history it would have rendered the whole of history a nonsense.

There would be no answer to the suffering of the innocent, of the oppressed, of all those forgotten in the vaults of history. If we lose this key to history, then we take the path to meaninglessness.

All *Rejoice Virgin Mother:*
        For Christ is risen.
        Alleluia.

Pr Only you, O Risen Christ, can bring us back to the joy of life. Only you can show us a tomb emptied from within. May we see our powerlessness when facing death without you. May we trust totally in the omnipotence of love, love which overcomes death.

R   *Amen*

All: *O Mary, temple of the Holy Spirit,*
         Guide us as witnesses of the Risen Lord
         In the way of Light

∾ THIRD STATION ∾

THE RISEN LORD APPEARS TO MARY MAGDALEN

'Woman, why are you weeping?'
'They have taken my Lord away' she replied
'and I don't know where they have put him.'

❧ THE RISEN LORD APPEARS TO ❧ MARY MAGDALEN

V *We adore you and bless you O Risen Lord*
R *Because by your death and resurrection you have given life to the world*

From the Gospel according to John

Meanwhile Mary stayed outside near the tomb, weeping. Then, still weeping, she stooped to look inside, and saw two angels in white sitting where the body of Jesus had been, one at the head, the other at the feet. 'They said, 'Woman, why are you weeping?' 'They have taken my Lord away' she replied 'and I don't know where they have put him.' As she said this she turned round and saw Jesus standing there, though she did not recognise him. Jesus said, 'Woman, why are you weeping? Who are you looking for?' Supposing him to be the gardener, she said, 'Sir, if you have taken him away, tell me where you have put him, and I will go and remove him'. Jesus said, 'Mary!' She knew him then and said to him in Hebrew, - 'Rabbuni!'- which means Master. Jesus said to her, 'Do not cling to me, because I have not yet ascended to the Father. But go and find the brothers, and tell them: I am ascending to my Father and your Father, to my God and your God.' So Mary of Magdala went and told the disciples that she had seen the Lord and that he had said these things to her. *(Jn 20:11-18)*

First Meditation

After returning to Jerusalem, John and Peter wait for news. Mary Magdalen alone, remains, and with eyes blurred by tears, she looks upon the tomb. She explains her sadness to the angel who question her: "They have taken him away". It is as though she is paralysed by her pain. Jesus, still unrecognised, calls her by name "Mary". Her face shines with joy, as her spirit is revived and her heart burns within her: it is he who has pronounced her name with his gentle voice and with his inimitable strength. Mary, called by her own name, answers with another name filled with all her affection and immense respect: "Master".

Second Meditation

Today's world still has much to learn. A woman, considered unworthy of listening to the scriptures, barred by law from giving witness, is chosen as the first witness of the resurrection. The whole of history begins to move in a new direction. The Risen Lord entrusts a woman with this vital task: to announce to the announcers the good news, to proclaim that life itself is alive; that the road closed to half of humankind, to woman, is finally opened. With the richness of her femininity, womankind becomes the repository of joy and of life in the Church. She is the new Eve for the new Millennium.

All *Rejoice Virgin Mother:*
For Christ is risen.
Alleluia.

Pr Risen Lord, you call me because you love me. In my daily life may I can recognise you as Mary Magdalen did. You say to me "Go and tell my brothers". Help me to travel the streets of this world, and carry out the great mission which is the proclamation of life, in my family, in school, in the office, in the factory, in the places where I spend my free time.

R *Amen*

All *O Mary, temple of the Holy Spirit,*
Guide us as witnesses of the Risen Lord
In the way of Light

❧ FOURTH STATION ❧
THE RISEN LORD APPEARS TO TWO DISCIPLES ON THE ROAD TO EMMAUS

*'...Was it not ordained that the Christ should
suffer and so enter into his glory?'*

❧ THE RISEN LORD APPEARS TO ❧ TWO DISCIPLES ON THE ROAD TO EMMAUS

V *We adore you and bless you O Risen Lord*
R *Because by your death and resurrection you have given life to the world*

From the Gospel according to Luke

That very same day, two of them were on their way to a village called Emmaus, seven miles from Jerusalem, and they were talking together about all that had happened. Now as they talked this over, Jesus himself came up and walked by their side; but something prevented them from recognising him. He said to them, 'What matters are you discussing as you walk along?' They stopped short, their faces downcast.

Then one of them, called Cleopas, answered him, 'You must be the only person staying in Jerusalem who does not know the things that have been happening there these last few days'. 'What things?' he asked. 'All about Jesus of Nazareth' they answered 'who proved he was a great prophet by the things he said and did in the sight of God and of the whole people; and how our chief priests and our leaders handed him over to be sentenced to death, and had him crucified. Our own hope had been that he would be the one to set Israel free. Then he said to them, 'You foolish men! So slow to believe the full message of the prophets! Was it not ordained that the Christ should suffer and so enter into his glory?' Then, starting with Moses and going through all the prophets, he explained to them the passages throughout the scriptures that were about himself. *(Lk 24:13-19, 25-27)*

First Meditation

'I am the Way' said Jesus. He is the path from God to man, meet by the dark side streets of a humanity that is wounded and increasingly divided. The meeting of ways between the radiant steps of Christ and the uncertain steps of man takes place on the road to Emmaus, on the morning of the Resurrection. The risen Lord, God's path to man, begins to become man's path to God. It was the day of light, but the disciples remained in their blindness. It was the day of joy but they remained in sadness. It was the day of the Resurrection, yet the disciples were as if dead. God pursues mankind as it walks on its way, because mankind is his chief concern. Jesus is God who veils himself at Emmaus; on the road he becomes our travelling companion. He does not force his entry, but knocks, waits, listens and asks. Then with patience he teaches us about himself.

Second Meditation

People of today are crushed by sorrow, weighed down by their affluence and possessions. There is however, a vast difference between the sorrow of the disciples on the road to Emmaus and our own. The disciples were sad because He was dead; we remain sad despite knowing that he lives. Faced with the events of our own lives, we remain paralysed. We have missed the crucial point. God accompanies us on our way, he guides us, chides us, and surprises us, empathizes with us, and yet we fail to trust in him. Jesus made as if to continue his journey with the two disciples. God's suggestions are an encouragement for us. His silence instead leaves us to take different roads, far from those we walked together with Him, roads which lead to doubt, discomfort and ultimately to disappointment.

All   *Rejoice Virgin Mother:*
For Christ is risen.
Alleluia.

Pr   Stay with us, Risen Lord, for evening comes. We will give you a home. We will offer you a place at our table. We will give you warmth. We will give you our love. Remain with us O Lord, for the dark night of doubt and disquiet seizes the heart of every man. Stay with us, Lord: and we will be near you; this is enough for us. Stay with us O Lord for evening comes. Make us witnesses of your resurrection

R   *Amen*

All   *O Mary, temple of the Holy Spirit,*
Guide us as witnesses of the Risen Lord
In the way of Light

∽ FIFTH STATION ∽
THE RISEN LORD REVEALS HIMSELF AT THE BREAKING OF BREAD

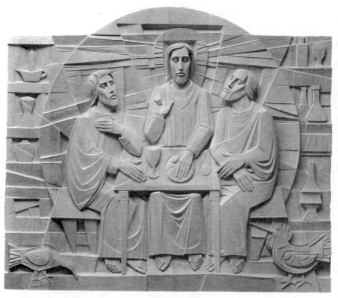

*'...he took the bread and said the blessing...
And their eyes were opened and
they recognised him...'*

❧ THE RISEN LORD REVEALS HIMSELF ❧
AT THE BREAKING OF BREAD

V   *We adore you and bless you O Risen Lord*
R   *Because by your death and resurrection you
have given life to the world*

From the Gospel according to Luke

When they drew near to the village to which they were
going, he made as if to go on; but they pressed him to
stay with them. 'It is nearly evening' they said 'and the
day is almost over.' So he went in to stay with them. Now
while he was with them at table, he took the bread and
said the blessing; then he broke it and handed it to them.
And their eyes were opened and they recognised him; but
he had vanished from their sight. Then they said to each
other, 'Did not our hearts burn within us as he talked to
us on the road and explained the scriptures to us?'

They set out that instant and returned to Jerusalem.
There they found the Eleven assembled together with their
companions, who said to them, 'Yes, it is true. The Lord
has risen and has appeared to Simon.' Then they told their
story of what had happened on the road and how they had
recognised him at the breaking of bread." (*Lk 24, 28-35*)

First Meditation

The Lord enters the Inn and, pressed to stay by the two disciples, he sits at table for the first time since the resurrection. It is the first meal of the heavenly Jesus, a foretaste of the eternal banquet of the Kingdom. Our destiny is this very banquet, communion with God and with God's children. The two disciples who have been instructed by the master along the road, through the scriptures, open their eyes at the breaking of bread. The result? Complete faith and an open heart. It is he, the Lord. Emmaus is a slow process of recognition. The master is our guide, leading us to the very heart of the word of God. Then there is his action, the enactment of the great Word; the banquet.

Second Meditation

Humanity has multiplied the means of communication, but has not opened the gates of its heart. It is necessary to attend the school of Emmaus. Every time we open the door of our heart to our neighbour, to a stranger, God opens his heart to us. The two disciples at Emmaus, performing an act of love, prepare themselves for the supreme experience of love: the banquet: they are open to knowing what love is: recognising Christ. If today's man began again to love those little ones, the poor, the marginalised, the oppressed, seeing in them children of God, only then, will the blindfolds be lifted from their eyes.

Then they will see love. They will experience the Risen Lord, God who waits for us by every road we take.

All   *Rejoice Virgin Mother:*
For Christ is risen.
Alleluia.

Pr   Risen Lord: in your last meal as an earthly man, you showed us, by washing the feet of your disciples, the only way of participating in the Eucharist. In your first meal as a heavenly man, you show us that in showing hospitality to the poor, lies the essence of communion with you. Lord of Glory, help us always to prepare our celebrations by washing the tired feet of those who are last, welcoming into our hearts and homes, all the "poor, the crippled, the lame, the blind," *(Lk 14:13)* those who are in need today, who have no distinguishing features except that of being your living image.

R   *Amen*

All   *O Mary, temple of the Holy Spirit,*
Guide us as witnesses of the Risen Lord
In the way of Light

❧ Sixth Station ❧
The Risen Lord Appears to His Disciples

*'Why are you so agitated,
and why are these doubts rising in your hearts?
Look at my hands and feet; yes, it is I indeed.'*

∞ THE RISEN LORD APPEARS TO ∞ HIS DISCIPLES

V *We adore you and bless you O Risen Lord*
R *Because by your death and resurrection you have given life to the world*

From the Gospel according to Luke

They were still talking about all this when he himself stood among them and said to them, 'Peace be with you!' In a state of alarm and fright, they thought they were seeing a ghost. But he said, 'Why are you so agitated, and why are these doubts rising in your hearts? Look at my hands and feet; yes, it is I indeed. Touch me and see for yourselves; a ghost has no flesh and bones as you can see I have.' And as he said this he showed them his hands and feet. Their joy was so great that they still could not believe it, and they stood there dumbfounded; so he said to them, 'Have you anything here to eat?' And they offered him a piece of grilled fish, which he took and ate before their eyes. (*Lk 24:36-43*)

First Meditation

The Risen Lord is a patient teacher, and he shows this in the upper room as he did on the road to Emmaus. Here we see a part of his Easter message: by word and deed he guides his own to believe the truth of the resurrection. He takes them from their initial fears to uncontrollable joy. "Touch me, and see for yourselves" (Lk 24:39). The word used by Christ denotes a tactile experience. It is the defining experience of the Christian message. John, in his first letter, uses the same word: "we have touched with our own hands: the Word, who is life" (1 Jn 1:1). The Risen Jesus is not a shadow. The resurrection is not a fairy tale. Easter is not a myth. The Risen Lord is alive, he is real. He is the true sign of the living God. He is the power of God's love. The Risen Lord represents mankind in his victory over death, something dreamed about by men of every age, but never accomplished. As he stands before us we find in him the beauty of a life that is not destined for corruption, a beauty we can touch like the flesh of a newborn baby. The world needs this Easter message.

Second Meditation

People today desire to meet those who will bear witness to the Risen Lord with their lives. The world wants to touch the scars of love, borne by the Church of the Risen Christ. To become such witnesses requires undergoing a process woven by patience, understanding, and the knowledge which is born of experience. We must acquaint ourselves with the risen Lord through prayer, the Word of God and the Eucharist. And we must not fail to be in tune with the world around us: with all its poverty and bewilderment, its anxieties and hopes for the future.

All   *Rejoice Virgin Mother:*
For Christ is risen.
Alleluia.

Pr   Risen Christ, we revere you for your patience in your Passion; for your silence. We revere you for your patience in your resurrection; for your teaching. Give to us, who are people of our own times, - people who want everything and who expect it 'now', - give us the gift of a love that knows how to wait, that can pause in prayer. You are alive, you are not a ghost. Give us the gift of knowing you as the 'Living One' *(Ap 1:18)*. Free us from the unreal images which we make of you. Make of us people ready to offer ourselves as signs of your resurrection, signs the world is waiting for in order to believe.

R   *Amen*

All   *O Mary, temple of the Holy Spirit,*
Guide us as witnesses of the Risen Lord
In the way of Light

≈ SEVENTH STATION ≈
THE RISEN LORD GIVES THE POWER TO FORGIVE SINS

'Receive the Holy Spirit. For those whose sins you forgive, they are forgiven; for those whose sins you retain, they are retained.'

≈ THE RISEN LORD GIVES ≈ THE POWER TO FORGIVE SINS

V *We adore you and bless you O Risen Lord*
R *Because by your death and resurrection you have given life to the world*

From the Gospel according to John

In the evening of that same day, the first day of the week, the doors were closed in the room where the disciples were, for fear of the Jews. Jesus came and stood among them. He said to them, 'Peace be with you', and showed them his hands and his side. The disciples were filled with joy when they saw the Lord, and he said to them again, 'Peace be with you. 'As the Father sent me, so am I sending you.' After saying this he breathed on them and said: 'Receive the Holy Spirit. For those whose sins you forgive, they are forgiven;for those whose sins you retain, they are retained.' (*Jn 20:19-23*)

First Meditation

The Holy Spirit is the first Easter gift of the Risen Lord, who now sits at the right hand of the Father. Together, the Father and his resurrected, only begotten Son, offer their greatest gift: the bond of their eternal love which is the Spirit, their

infinite kiss, their reciprocal joy, their feast of pure light. The
Spirit is symbolised by breath, the breath of life which flows
from the depths of our being, just as the Spirit streams forth
from the heart of the shared life of the Father and the Son.
For this reason the Risen Lord announces his peace, his
shalom: which is the remission of sins. The Spirit is the per-
fect harmony between the Father and the Son.

"God loved the world so much that he gave his only
Son" *(Jn 3:16)*. The Father and his Risen Son so loved
the world that they gave their Spirit. Here we encounter
the heart of love, which gives and forgives.

Second Meditation

People today need life. The whole world is in need of the
Holy Spirit which is the life and peace of the Father, Son
and Spirit. We are forever searching for pleasure in our
lives but we have lost the true joy of life. This world has
snuffed out so many unborn lives, losing what is the true
meaning of life. Despite endless new means of communication, we live in cold anonymity, unable to break
through to others. We have increased the world's income,
but two thirds of the world suffers in abject poverty. The
hunger for possessions in the wealthy north has caused a
famine of goods in the poverty stricken south.
Nevertheless, Resurrection is possible. The Church of the
Risen Lord has the power to forgive our sins of selfish-
ness, sins from hearts that are closed toward the needy.

All *Rejoice Virgin Mother:*
For Christ is risen.
Alleluia.

Pr Come Holy Spirit. You, the first gift of the Risen Lord. May you fill us with the enthusiasm of the Father and the Son, lest we sink in the darkness and boredom of our lives. Harmony of the Father and the Son, guide us towards justice and peace: free us from the chains of death. Eternal life of the Father and the Son, breathe into these dry bones and let us pass from sin to grace. Youth of the Father and the Son, make us ever young, willing and able announcers of the Resurrection.

R *Amen*

All *O Mary, temple of the Holy Spirit,*
Guide us as witnesses of the Risen Lord
In the way of Light

❧ Eighth Station ❧
The Lord Confirms
the Faith of Thomas

'You believe because you can see me.
Happy are those who have not seen
and yet believe.'

❧ THE LORD CONFIRMS ❧
THE FAITH OF THOMAS

V   *We adore you and bless you O Risen Lord*
R   *Because by your death and resurrection you have given life to the world*

From the Gospel according to John

Thomas, called the Twin, who was one of the Twelve, was not with them when Jesus came. When the disciples said, 'We have seen the Lord', he answered, 'Unless I see the holes that the nails made in his hands and can put my finger into the holes they made, and unless I can put my hand into his side, I refuse to believe'. Eight days later the disciples were in the house again and Thomas was with them. The doors were closed, but Jesus came in and stood among them. 'Peace be with you' he said. Then he spoke to Thomas, 'Put your finger here; look, here are my hands. Give me your hand; put it into my side.' Doubt no longer but believe.' Thomas replied, 'My Lord and my God!' Jesus said to him:'You believe because you can see me. Happy are those who have not seen and yet believe.' *(Jn 20:24-29)*

First Meditation

Thomas the doubter is led by the hand to touch the wounds of a dead man who is risen. He touches, prostrates himself and exclaims "My Lord and my God!" Those scars are the credentials of God, they are the signature of God in the life of Jesus of Nazareth. They are the seal on all that he said, beginning from his own self affirmation "I am the Way, the Truth and the Life... The Father and I are One" *(Jn 14:6; 10:30)*. With Thomas, the entire world touches the true sign of the Living God. He was invited to touch Christ's wounds on behalf of us all. And he was healed from his own wounds of incredulity. Through this exchange, our wounds too, are healed, and faith is reborn.

Second Meditation

People today who are so used to believing only what they can see with their own eyes, need Thomas's experience. Also today Christ says to us: 'touch me' in the Church, in the Saints. The task of spreading the signs of the resurrection is entrusted to us believers. Through a renewed commitment to the culture of Life, inspired by the life of the Spirit growing within us, and in the name of the Lord who has emerged victorious over death, we can promote life in all its splendour. The Church of believers will only be credible in the 'upper rooms' of today, if she can present to the world martyrs and servants, 'wounds' that can be touched. Only then will she be believed.

All *Rejoice Virgin Mother:*
For Christ is risen.
Alleluia.

Pr Risen Lord, in faith we say to you each day, "my Lord and my God". Faith is not the final response to what we see. To have Faith is not easy, but it brings us happiness. To have faith is to trust in you even when we find ourselves in darkness. To have faith is to entrust ourselves to you during trials and tribulations. Lord of life, increase our faith. Give us the faith that is rooted in your passion. Give us the trust that is the flowering of Easter. Give us the faithfulness which is the fruit of Easter.

R *Amen*

All *O Mary, temple of the Holy Spirit,*
Guide us as witnesses of the Risen Lord
In the way of Light

≈ NINTH STATION ≈
THE RISEN LORD MEETS HIS DISCIPLES ON THE SHORE OF GALILEE

*'So they dropped the net, and there were
so many fish that they could not haul it in.'*

∼ THE RISEN LORD MEETS HIS ∼ DISCIPLES ON THE SHORE OF GALILEE

V   *We adore you and bless you O Risen Lord*
R   *Because by your death and resurrection you have given life to the world*

From the Gospel according to John

Later on, Jesus showed himself again to the disciples. It was by the Sea of Tiberias, and it happened like this: Simon Peter, Thomas called the Twin, Nathanael from Cana in Galilee, the sons of Zebedee and two more of his disciples were together. Simon Peter said, 'I'm going fishing'. They replied, 'We'll come with you'. They went out and got into the boat but caught nothing that night.

It was light by now and there stood Jesus on the shore, though the disciples did not realise that it was Jesus. Jesus called out, 'Have you caught anything, friends?' And when they answered, 'No', he said, 'Throw the net out to starboard and you'll find something'. So they dropped the net, and there were so many fish that they could not haul it in. The disciple Jesus loved said to Peter, 'It is the Lord'. At these words 'It is the Lord', Simon Peter, who had practically nothing on, wrapped his cloak round him and jumped into the water. The other disciples came on in the boat, towing the net and the fish; they were only about a hundred yards from land.

As soon as they came ashore they saw that there was some bread there, and a charcoal fire with fish cooking on it. Jesus then stepped forward, took the bread and gave it to them, and the same with the fish. (*Jn 21:1-9, 13*)

First Meditation

Jesus asks for food even though he needs nothing, for his risen body is already glorious. He asks in order to continue to share in the needs of mankind, to share in their daily bread. As he did at the well of Sikar when he asked the Samaritan woman for water. A God who asks is indeed unique. He asks of mankind so that God can enter into our world, and respond to it with the power of his love. He questions his disciples in order to coax them into throwing their nets into the deep. The very same nets that once remained obstinately empty are now prodigiously full. Christ then invites the disciples to a joyful and plentiful meal. Without him, the table would have been miserable and bare.

Second Meditation

Jesus knocks at our door today. He wants to enter into a world that is weary and in despair, full of bright lights but lacking the one true light. We live in a world full of successes that are enjoyed only by a few. Yet its heart remains as empty as the nets. All around us there is poverty, oppression, and dehumanisation, with the future closed to so many. Stomachs remain as empty as the nets on that morning, allowing mankind to taste the emptiness of both soul and body; the absence of the divine and absence of the human. Jesus, risen from the dead, draws near and speaks. When God loves, he gives freely to us. When God holds especially dear then he asks from us. He asks us to rediscover hope and love, virtues we gain through practise.

All *Rejoice Virgin Mother:*
For Christ is risen.
Alleluia.

Pr Risen Lord, make us to ready to put our trust in you despite all our many failures. You, the Risen one sit at table to eat with us. In the days of the Easter season, you stayed among us not showing yourself as a triumphal God amidst thunder and lightning but as a simple God who celebrates the resurrection on the shores of a lake, at a table with us. Make us witnesses of your resurrection, in the tedium of our everyday lives, where you wait to meet us, on the shores of our labours. Sit together with us every day as we eat our fill but remain empty. Sit always at the tables of the poor who still have hope in you. Then will the world be renewed in the image of your Resurrection.

R *Amen*

All *O Mary, temple of the Holy Spirit,*
Guide us as witnesses of the Risen Lord
In the way of Light

❧ TENTH STATION ❧
THE RISEN LORD CONFERS PRIMACY ON PETER

'Lord, you know everything;
you know I love you'.
Jesus said to him, 'Feed my sheep'.

∼ THE RISEN LORD CONFERS ∼ PRIMACY ON PETER

V   *We adore you and bless you O Risen Lord*
R   *Because by your death and resurrection you have given life to the world*

From the Gospel according to John

After the meal Jesus said to Simon Peter, 'Simon son of John, do you love me more than these others do?' He answered, 'Yes Lord, you know I love you'. Jesus said to him, 'Feed my lambs'. A second time he said to him, 'Simon son of John, do you love me?' He replied, 'Yes, Lord, you know I love you'. Jesus said to him, 'Look after my sheep'. Then he said to him a third time, 'Simon son of John, do you love me?' Peter was upset that he asked him the third time, 'Do you love me?' and said, 'Lord, you know everything; you know I love you'. Jesus said to him, 'Feed my sheep'. *(Jn 21:15-17)*

First Meditation

The Risen Lord meets Peter. The quiet lapping waves of the lake on which Peter is heard in the background. Jesus speaks with him heart to heart. After the great encounter,

the great task is assigned. Three times the Lord looks for a
declaration of love: "Simon Peter, do you love me more
than these others do?" Only days before, he had denied
Jesus. Three times reparation had to be made for that
betrayal of love, by a renewed declaration of that love.
"You know everything Lord, you know that I love you."
And with each statement of love from Peter, Jesus bestows
those powers which are at the service of love: "feed my
sheep, feed my lambs". To love Jesus above all things, is
not 'beautiful ideal': it is a service to those whom Christ
holds dearest, to those he paid for with his blood.

Second Meditation

People of our own times, buffeted as they are by winds
and storms, need a secure and steadfast reference point
now more than ever. We need the certainty that is Christ:
Christ who feeds his sheep and his lambs through Peter,
whose mission is to feed and nourish, to feed and illumi-
nate, to feed and comfort, to feed and free us. To feed and
make us grow. Peter is an Easter gift, he is one of us, a
brother, who was made shepherd not because of his
humanity which was as fragile as that of any of us, but by
the word of Christ who sustains him. In the name of
Jesus, He acts as our guide, for all who are the sheep of
his flock.

All *Rejoice Virgin Mother:*
For Christ is risen.
Alleluia.

Pr We thank you Risen Christ for the Peter of today, for our Pope, who lives his apostolic service with such generosity, warmth and sacrifice for this world in which so many opportunities and so many hardships. Every day you put the same question to us as well: "Do you love me more than these others?" Together with Peter and under his guidance, you give us a part of your flock to tend. We in turn entrust ourselves to you. Teach us, Master and giver of life, that we will feed your flock only if we love, and that only through sacrifice, will we nourish that flock with your truth and your peace.

R *Amen*

All *O Mary, temple of the Holy Spirit,*
Guide us as witnesses of the Risen Lord
In the way of Light

≈ ELEVENTH STATION ≈
THE RISEN LORD ENTRUSTS TO HIS DISCIPLES THE MISSION TO THE WORLD

'Go, therefore, make disciples of all the nations.'

THE RISEN LORD ENTRUSTS TO HIS DISCIPLES THE MISSION TO THE WORLD

V *We adore you and bless you O Risen Lord*

R *Because by your death and resurrection you have given life to the world*

From the Gospel according to Matthew

Meanwhile the eleven disciples set out for Galilee, to the mountain where Jesus had arranged to meet them. When they saw him they fell down before him, though some hesitated. Jesus came up and spoke to them. He said, 'All authority in heaven and on earth has been given to me. Go, therefore, make disciples of all the nations; baptise them in the name of the Father and of the Son and of the Holy Spirit, and teach them to observe all the commands I gave you. And know that I am with you always; yes, to the end of time.' *(Mt 28:16-20)*

First Meditation

The Risen Jesus is the Lord of History. The power given him by the Father he passes on to his own. On Mount Galilee he inaugurates a new chapter in that history, just as he did on the Mount of the Beatitudes. There at

Galilee, the Lord showed us the new DNA of mankind who is made of flesh but imbued with the Spirit and given the mission to change the face of the Earth. To baptise and to divinise mankind, each and every fragile creature. To instruct and shed light on the new destiny of the world. To make disciples of all nations, of every race and culture and bring them into the Easter people, the Church. This communion is the sign and dwelling place of Trinitarian love, a dwelling place to which all are called. This mission, this mandate is an immense calling, which demands complete dedication to the good news. At Easter this impetus does not end, it only begins. The field, the vineyard is the whole world, until the end of time.

Second Meditation

People of today live in the immense 'field' of the world. It is a world that becomes ever more complex with ever increasing needs and crises; the dangers of war, and suffering caused by senseless violence. What is our work in this world? How can we proclaim the good news? How can we bring about change peacefully? How can we remain faithful to the Lord of History and to the History of salvation? We can, because the Risen Lord is with us, until the end of time.

All *Rejoice Virgin Mother:*
For Christ is risen.
Alleluia.

Pr Lord, we hear your promise: "know that I am with you always" *(Mt 28,20)* and we are comforted. We are unable to carry even the lightest burden alone for long. Still less can we carry on our poor shoulders the weight of this world. We are weak, while you Lord, are strength. We are fickle, while you Lord, are constant. We are fearful, while you Lord, are courage. We are sadness, while you Lord are joy. We are the night, while you Lord, are the light. We remain motionless while, you Lord, are the Resurrection.

R *Amen*

All *O Mary, temple of the Holy Spirit,*
Guide us as witnesses of the Risen Lord
In the way of Light

❧ TWELFTH STATION ❧
THE RISEN LORD ASCENDS
TO THE FATHER

' *...Jesus who has been taken up from you into
heaven, this same Jesus will come back in the
same way as you have seen him go there.*'

⇜ THE RISEN LORD ASCENDS ⇝
TO THE FATHER

V   *We adore you and bless you O Risen Lord*
R   *Because by your death and resurrection you*
       have given life to the world

A Reading from the Acts of the Apostles

Now having met together, they asked him, 'Lord, has the
time come? Are you going to restore the kingdom to
Israel?' He replied, 'It is not for you to know times or
dates that the Father has decided by his own authority,
but you will receive power when the Holy Spirit comes
on you,' and then you will be my witnesses not only in
Jerusalem but throughout Judaea and Samaria, and indeed
to the ends of the earth'.

As he said this he was lifted up while they looked on,
and a cloud took him from their sight. They were still
staring into the sky when suddenly two men in white
were standing near them and they said, 'Why are you
men from Galilee standing here looking into the sky?
Jesus who has been taken up from you into heaven, this
same Jesus will come back in the same way as you have
seen him go there.'*(Ac 1:6-11)*

First Meditation

The Risen Lord is victorious upon death. He has entered
into everlasting life. His very body is marked with the
signs of glory. During the forty days of Easter he allows
himself to be seen, touched, embraced; he speaks, walks
and eats with his own, and to them he gives his final
supreme promise: "You will have the power of the Holy
Spirit" to bring about the universal mission. The cry on
the cross "all is accomplished" now becomes true in all
its fullness. As he enters into everlasting life, the Risen
Lord removes himself from the ordinary gaze of our fragile eyes. But the Risen Lord remains with us as he said he
would: "I am with you always; yes, to the end of time".
Jesus now shares with the Father his universal Kingship.
He sits at God's right hand and mankind enters into the
realm of God. No atheist could ever raise matter to such
heights. Never was matter itself so glorified as in the
mystey of the Ascension of our Risen Lord.

Second Meditation

People today do not look up into the heavens; the earth is
enough for them. Heaven, however, is the mode of being
of the invisible God. The saints share in it as sons and
co-heirs. Mankind however, blinded by materialism and
the need to have goods, pleasure and power, does not
focus on the invisible reality. We suffer from chronic
short-sightedness, if not total blindness. Mankind is

afraid that to look heavenward means to forget the earth. Instead heaven will be the final reward for those who on earth gave food to the hungry, comfort to those in despair. Only those who gave a taste of heaven in this world to the poor and hungry and children of God, will enter the heaven of the eternal resurrection.

All *Rejoice Virgin Mother:*
For Christ is risen.
Alleluia.

Pr Risen Lord, you went ahead to prepare a place for us. The rightful place of mankind as sons of God is at the right hand of God the Father in all his maternal love. Our place has been purchased by you, and it is now for us not to squander it. Let our eyes be fixed on where there is eternal joy. A taste of paradise can change everything. As we look forward to the fullness of Easter that is yet to come, we commit ourselves to making the Resurrection present for every person and for humanity itself. Today's Easter, which sets mankind free, is the joyful herald of eternal blessedness.

R *Amen*

All *O Mary, temple of the Holy Spirit,*
Guide us as witnesses of the Risen Lord
In the way of Light

～ THIRTEENTH STATION ～
WAITING FOR THE HOLY SPIRIT WITH MARY THE MOTHER OF JESUS

*'...All these joined in continuous prayer,
together with several women,
including Mary the mother of Jesus.'*

❧ WAITING FOR THE HOLY SPIRIT ❧ WITH MARY THE MOTHER OF JESUS

V *We adore you and bless you O Risen Lord*
R *Because by your death and resurrection you have given life to the world*

A reading from the Acts of the Apostles

So from the Mount of Olives, as it is called, they went back to Jerusalem, a short distance away, no more than a sabbath walk; and when they reached the city they went to the upper room where they were staying; there were Peter and John, James and Andrew, Philip and Thomas, Bartholomew and Matthew, James son of Alphaeus and Simon the Zealot, and Jude son of James. All these joined in Continuous prayer, together with several women, including Mary the mother of Jesus, and with his brothers. (*Acts 1:12-14*)

First Meditation

Waiting for the Holy Spirit. Having come down from the mountain, they begin to pray. Jesus is no longer visible. The cloud of the Ascension has fixed his place in glory. The Risen Lord, no longer visible to our human eyes, can now only be seen with the eyes of faith. The Easter people invites the Holy Spirit. His coming is eagerly awaited, for in the fullness of all his gifts he will bring about the birth of the Church, and guide its first steps on the way to becoming the emissary of his resurrection. The invocation of the Holy Spirit is always efficacious. This was guaranteed by Christ when he said: "If you then, who are evil, know how to give your children what is good, how much more will the heavenly Father give the Holy Spirit to those who ask him" *(Lk 11:13)*. From this moment on the Easter people is united in the name of the Risen Lord. With Him in our midst, we implore the Father for the Holy Spirit of love, who renews the face of the Earth. Then will come an eternal Pentecost. The Easter prayer is marked by the presence of Mary, the mother of Jesus; she was present from the beginning at Cana, where people first began to believe in his signs; she was present at Calvary where the Church was gestated, and now she is present in the Upper Room, where the Church is born. Mary the mother of Jesus: she who knows best the Easter mysteries: death and life, cross and resurrection.

Second Meditation

People of today are so distracted by the materialism that surrounds them that they are fooled into forgetting God and taking into paths that lead only to death. Yet, a light shines out at the turning point of this age: it is the Church, which Christ founded to save those in search of salvation. It is the Church, gathered in prayer, harmony and perseverance. It is the Church, twenty centuries young who speaks to those who are young in spirit. The philosophy of the world runs counter to the beatitudes, and draws mankind further and further away from God. The Church instead radiates the light of Christ himself and brings mankind back to God. The way of the Upper Room leads us to the culture of life.

All   *Rejoice Virgin Mother:*
          For Christ is risen.
          Alleluia.

Pr   Christ, you who have risen from the dead, and who are ever present in your Paschal community, through the intercession of your Mother who is with us still, pour out on us the Holy Spirit. Your Spirit, the Spirit of your ever loving Father: the Spirit of life, Spirit of joy, Spirit of peace, of strength, of love, the Spirit of the Resurrection.

R   *Amen*

All   *O Mary, temple of the Holy Spirit,*
          Guide us as witnesses of the Risen Lord
          In the way of Light

❧ FOURTEENTH STATION ❧
THE RISEN LORD SENDS THE SPIRIT
PROMISED TO THE DISCIPLES

*'They were all filled with the Holy Spirit,
and began to speak foreign languages as the
Spirit gave them the gift of speech.'*

❧ THE RISEN LORD SENDS THE SPIRIT ❧ PROMISED TO THE DISCIPLES

V   *We adore you and bless you O Risen Lord*
R   *Because by your death and resurrection you*
       have given life to the world

A reading from the Acts of the Apostles

When Pentecost day came round, they had all met in one room, when suddenly they heard what sounded like a powerful wind from heaven, the noise of which filled the entire house in which they were sitting; and something appeared to them that seemed like tongues of fire; these separated and came to rest on the head of each of them. They were all filled with the Holy Spirit, and began to speak foreign languages as the Spirit gave them the gift of speech.

Now there were devout men living in Jerusalem from every nation under heaven, and at this sound they all assembled, each one bewildered to hear these men speaking his own language.' *(Ac 2:1-6)*

First Meditation

Pentecost is a promise kept. The Risen Lord fulfills his solemn promise: "The Advocate, the Holy Spirit, whom

the Father will send in my name" *(Jn 14:26)*. God is
faithful. He honours his commitments. He said: the Son
of Man will "give his life as a ransom for many" *(Mt
20:28)*, and his word became incarnate on Good Friday.
He said "destroy this sanctuary, and in three days I will
raise it up...". He spoke of the sanctuary that was his body
(Jn 2:19.21), and the Word was victorious upon death.
He said "you will receive power when the Holy Spirit
comes on you" *(Ac 1:8)*, and when the seven weeks of
Easter had ended, his word was 'Pentecost': the power of
the Holy Spirit, and the birth of the Church. A new
humanity begins on its journey.

Second Meditation

People today must remember that "the true nature of sin,
is to be unresponsive to the Holy Spirit". That is to say,
closed to love. The Spirit defeats our pessimism for God
looks on humanity with optimism. The Holy Spirit is the
power behind all good things: good works, love winning
through, the ripening of the wheat field. Pentecost unites
the whole of mankind. To believe in the Holy Spirit,
even for the tired sceptic within us, means not only to
believe in God's love for me, but to trust that God
believes in me, that God has faith in me, that God
expects much from me. I must allow myself to be swept
along by the Spirit who is even now working in history.
Then life will truly be a coming together of love and

peace. "What the Spirit brings... is love, joy, peace, patience, kindness, goodness, trustfulness gentleness and self control." *(Gal 5:22)*

All *Rejoice Virgin Mother:*
For Christ is risen.
Alleluia.

Pr O Holy Spirit, ineffable bond between the Father and the Son; it is you who unites us with Christ Risen. You are the breath of our life. It is you who unites us to the Church, whose soul you are, and whose body we constitute. Like St Augustine each one of us begs of you:

All *Breathe in me, O Holy Spirit, that my thoughts*
may all be holy.
Act in me, O Holy Spirit,
that my work, too, may be holy.
Draw my heart, O Holy Spirit,
that I may love but what is holy.
Strengthen me, O Holy Spirit, to defend all
that is holy. Guard me, then, O Holy Spirit,
that I always may be holy.

R *Amen*

All *O Mary, temple of the Holy Spirit,*
Guide us as witnesses of the Risen Lord
In the way of Light

Conclusion

The celebrant invites all the participants to light a candle from the Paschal candle, while he reads the following saying to each person or to the whole assembly:

Pr   Go and take the light of the Risen Lord to the people whom you meet.

R   *Amen*

(All renew baptismal promises.)

Pr   Baptism is our participation in Christ's resurrection. Let us conclude our journey, renewing our baptismal promises, grateful to the Father who continues to call us from the darkness to the light of his Kingdom

Brothers and sisters, if you wish to follow the Risen Lord in the nidst of the world

Do you reject sin, so as to live in the freedom of God's children?

R   *I do.*

Pr   Do you reject the glamour of evil, and refuse to be mastered by sin?

R   *I do.*

Pr Do you reject Satan, father of sin and prince of darkness?

R *I do.*

Pr Do you believe in God, the Father Almighty, creator of heaven and earth?

R *I do.*

Pr Do you believe in Jesus Christ, his only Son, our Lord, who was born of the Virgin Mary, was crucified, died, and was buried, rose from the dead, and is now seated at the right hand of the Father?

R *I do.*

Pr Do you believe in the Holy Spirit, the holy Catholic Church, the communion of saints, the forgiveness of sins, the resurrection of the body, and life everlasting?

R *I do.*

Pr God, the all-powerful Father of our Lord Jesus Christ, has given us a new birth by water and the Holy Spirit, and forgiven all our sins. May he also keep us faithful to our Lord Jesus Christ for ever and ever.

R *Amen.*

(*Final Hymn*)